— HELP WANTED/CATS —

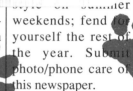

SIAMESE CAT WANTED

o "cry" in background while I telephone my mother, so he'll think I've had a baby. Then when I ell her it's just a cat he'll be so relieved he'll get off my ack about this whole marriage hing. Please leave essage and crying emonstration on my nswering machine.

RE YOU READING HIS?

f so, you're too mart to work for a owl of water at the nd of a maze. Sorry. f you know any umb cats who want further the cause f our unnecessary esearch, tell them to ontact us at box 904 care of this magane.

I WILL PAY TOP DOLLAR

for a reliable cat to use the sandbox, if you know what I mean, of the bratty two-year-old who lives next door to me. Double overtime for any "visits" after ten at night, plus taxi fare home. Sizeable bonus if/when the family moves away.

SOUS-CHEF JOB AVAILABLE

to work weekend at small country inn. Prefer CIA grad with some patisserie experience. Must have at least — oops, we're advertising in the wrong magazine. The Health Inspector would never let us hire a cat for this job.

WANT TO MAKE EXTRA MONEY AT HOME?

Look no further. Directors of writing school for would-be children's authors need reliable manuscript scuffers to make it look as though we've actually read the manuscripts ourselves. Pay is $1.00/page—plus the knowledge that you're furthering a creative endeavor. No clawing, please. Submit some sample scuffed-up pages to Box 8794.

HUGE FORTUNES AWAIT

dedicated Kitty-Litter-kickers. Call 752-555-2607 to find out how you can get a piece of this incredible opportunity.

SEEK FELINE ENTREPRENEU

to inve
Mor, a
and-fle
program
is guaranteed to dou ble in five years, provided we are still in business. Box 59

FAT CATS

and kittens need help. Sensitive, experienced camp counselors wanted to staff Pretty Kitty, a lakeside weight camp for cats. Pay is good; surroundings are spectacular; food is horrible generic dry stuff served out of bags. But hey—you could probably stand to take off a couple of pounds yourself, right? Send resumes to Box 26.

DECORATIVE CAT

needed he C ng rn in style on summer weekends; fend for yourself the rest of the year. Submit photo/phone care of this newspaper.

WE'RE TIRED OF UNROLLING RUGS

and having mouse nests fall out onto the customers' feet. Carpet store seeks an experienced mouser at least a year old. You must be unobtrusive and capable of consuming the whole mouse without leaving any leftover "presents" for us to find. Pay is $8 a week; you'll catch your own food, of course. Great benefits, including free shots and some nice

√501

Date Due

AUG 20 '97			
DEC 12 '97			
DEC 22 '98			
2-1-99			

8/97

Hard Times for Cats!

Ann Hodgman

Abbeville Press · Publishers

New York · London · Paris

Editor: Susan Costello
Designer: Celia Fuller
Production Supervisor: Hope Koturo
Production Editor: Sarah Key
Picture Researcher: Anne Manning

page 1: **Mummy, how do you spell 'litter-trained'?**
▪ Perfect spelling is as crucial on cat resumes as it
is on human ones, and an unabridged dictionary
can come in very handy. "See, honey? It's 'mice,'
not 'mouses,'" a Scottish Fold mother points out to
her kitten, who is applying for his first job at only
eight weeks.

page 2: **Taking time to smell the dandelions** ▪
"Nature's pretty cool," comments a half-grawn
shorthair during a family trip to the Dakota
prairies. "When I worked in the city I never had
time for this stuff, but now I'm really starting to
appreciate flowers and insects and stuff like that.
'Course if I get another job I'm not going to tell
anyone that—they'd think I'd flaked out on them."

pages 4–5: **Clawing through the want ads** ▪
Twins Mabel and Sable are desperately seeking a
job for two. They were last employed at a broker-
age as security cats.

Library of Congress Cataloging-in-Publication Data
Hodgman, Ann.
Hard times for cats! / Ann Hodgman.
p. cm.
ISBN 1-55859-395-0
1. Cats—Humor. 2. American wit and humor.
I. Title.
PN6231.C23H64 1992
818'.5402—dc20   92-164 56
CIP

Compilation copyright ©Abbeville Press, Inc.

Printed and bound in Hong Kong
First edition

· Contents ·

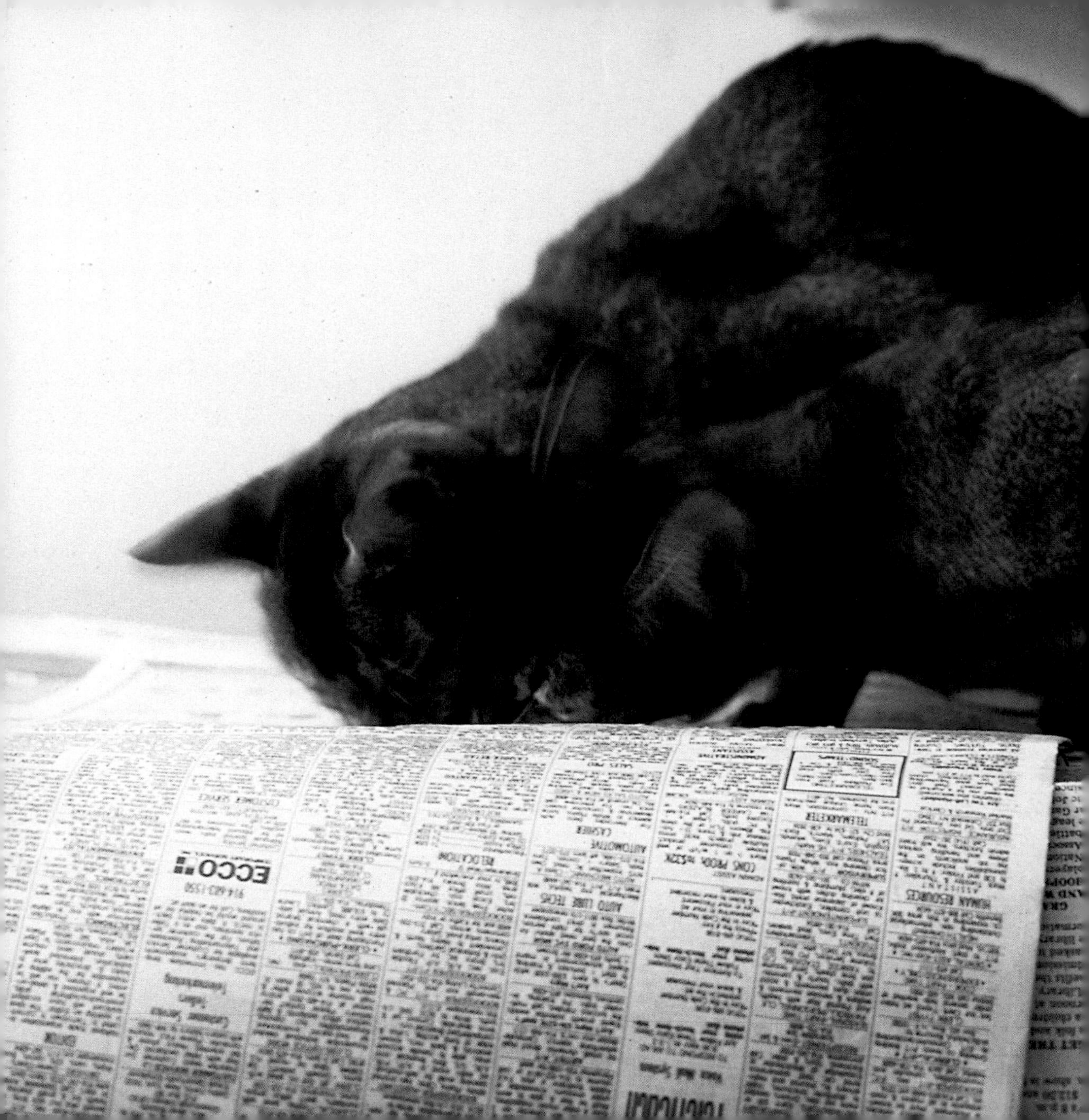
ECCO

· The Unemployed Cat ·

Poor cats. Just because they like hunting rodents, we expect them to work for us. "Look!" we think. "An animal with a useful trait! Let's domesticate it and then enslave it." (I'm not exactly sure why we think a cat's ability to spread a vole's entrails over our back steps is useful, but we'll let that pass.) Before the cat can even unsheathe its claws, we've given it a social security number and started docking it for lateness.

Catching mice is the least of it, too. In ancient Egypt, cats worked as gods, a great job if you can get it, but that was the high point of their career history. Later on, they had much less happy occupations as the butt of medieval Europeans' yucky superstitions.

Apparently these jobs consisted mainly of spoiling humans' jobs and being hated for it. In medieval France, for example, cats were believed to prevent bakers' bread from rising and to wreck the catch for fishermen. Of course we now realize that the medieval French were a little bit eccentric—and yet anyone who's ever tried to prepare for a dinner party with a cat sandbagging itself around his ankles will acknowledge that cats do have an almost supernatural ability to get in the way when you're in a hurry. Perhaps some of these old superstitions are truer than we think.

Medieval cats were also expected to "work" in the medical arts, largely by donating parts of themselves that they would probably have preferred to hang onto. It was said that the blood from a tomcat's tail could cure the injuries of someone who had fallen; cats' ears in red wine could cure pneumonia; fresh cats' brains could turn people invisible; and cat stew could cause human women to have kittens. Do the last two count as medical procedures? I guess so—at least for the cat.

Not surprisingly, cats' lives became more pleasant once Western civilization stopped thinking of them as witches' accessories. More pleasant from a physical point of view, that is. The many cats who found jobs inspiring writers must have been mortified by the quantities of *bad* cat-related writing their owners turned out. Take, for example, the poet Christopher Smart's paeon to his cat Jeoffrey, written in 1763:

> For I will consider my Cat Jeoffrey.
> For he is the servant of the Living God duly and daily serving him.
> For at the first glance at the glory of God in the East he worships in his way.
> For this is done by wreathing his body seven times round with elegant quickness.
> For he leaps up to catch the musk, which is the blessing of God upon his prayer. . . .

And so on and so on, all the way down to "For he is of the tribe of Tiger."

Smart was a madman, of course, and thus perhaps shouldn't be held up to the same scrutiny as a *real* writer. Even the usually reliable Keats, however, composed a—well—not-so-good sonnet about the cat of his friend John Hamilton Reynalds; the worst lines, I think, are these:

Pr'thee do not stick
Thy latent talons in me—and unpraise
Thy gentle mew—and tell me all the frays
Of fish and mice, and rats and tender chick.
Nay, look not down, nor lick thy dainty
wrists—
For all the wheezy asthma . . .

Some years later, Thomas Hardy wrote a cat poem ("Lines to a Dumb Friend") whose opening couplet's awfulness has never been surpassed: "Pet was never mourned as you,/Purrer of the spotless hue."

As the twentieth century dawned and people forgot how to read, more and more cats found themselves fired from the task of making good writers write badly. The pluckier among them managed to find work in the comic strips: among others,

Felix in the "Felix the Cat" series, by Otto Messmer, Pat Sullivan Studio, from *Too Funny for Words: Disney's Greatest Sight Gags.*

Krazy Kat, Heathcliffe, Garfield, and Fritz. Here the pay was fine, but money hardly compensates for the knowledge that one is a negative role model. (Actually it compensates pretty well, but it's got to be stressful pretending that you don't *think* it does.) Nastiest role model of all was the Cat in the Hat, a sub-cartoon character whose horrifying antics gave ulcers to a whole generation of Sputnik-era first-graders and got cats everywhere into trouble when they tried to balance fishbowls on the points of umbrellas.

Now that the world, or at least the United States, appears to have given up reading entirely, some intrepid cats are looking to television for work. Unfortunately, Morris used up all the jobs in TV before he died or retired or whatever he did. But now that he's safely out of the

way, new jobs as Morris impersonators may give cats in the future something to reach for.

I haven't even mentioned all the unsung employed cats: the humble, ordinary creatures who held lowly jobs chasing moths in laundromats and sitting in the ticket windows at Off-Off Broadway theaters and playing with peoples' shoelaces at shoeshine stands. The reason I haven't is that—well, the recession came along. They're all out of work now, and more unsung than ever. For many of them, that's not so bad: I'm sure we all know cats who, if they don't feel like working in the first place, *don't.* For the rest, being unemployed is just as painful as it is for humans; perhaps it's even more so, since an out-of-work cat can't collect unemployment or go bowling.

He or she—or "gender-free," as the two neutered cats in my household always like to remind me—can do a lot of other things to pass the time, though. One of them, of course, is giving interviews. Herewith we salute the job-hunting cats who put down the want ads long enough to share their fears, their dreams, and their grooming tips with us. Hard times have made them so cooperative and so polite that we can't help hoping these cats never find work again.

·1·
Feline Firings:
The Low-Down
on Layoffs

**People aren't the only
mammals to lose their jobs**

◄◄ Moving day · It hurts when you're moved out of the office in a packing carton. "Couldn't they at least have used the 9-Lives box?" asked Smokey mournfully.

◄ Laid off by *la municipalité* · The specter of unemployment haunts cats worldwide. Minette, who had worked happily at this French municipal hall for seven years, here stands at loose ends after having discovered a *bout rose* (pink slip) in her water dish. Her remarks on her plight were untranslatable.

► No more work in Napa Valley · "I'm not worried," Kirby claims, although his prospects of finding another winery job are slim. "You know, mice are incredible lushes. They *love* wine. When a couple of customers open their wine bottles and find Squeaky floating around inside, my boss will be *begging* me to come back."

◄ Laid off by a San Francisco bookstore · "They claim they're computerizing," was the tearful report of a calico cat who was fired from her job at a San Francisco book store. "They don't need me to tell them which books to order or return—as if a *computer* would know to send back all those dog books! So they put me out on the street. I mean, it may be Haight Street, but it's still the *street!* I'll show them. I'll sell art books on the sidewalk in front of the store.

◄ **Don't call us . . .** · When this office closed, Kelby found herself packed up along with the furniture. "So this is what fate does to you," the still-stunned animal mused from her new home— a warehouse. "You give your whole life to the company, and you end up sleeping on a pile of old mailing envelopes."

► **I know they're in there** · "They *can't* have left," jabbers a panic-stricken shorthair. "A whole business *couldn't* shut down with no warning! They're just—they're just planning a surprise party for me. That's it, a surprise party . . ."

► Restaurant reductions · "The minute I'd finished drying the dishes, the chef let me go. I wish I'd dried them with my tail."

◄ No more work at the trattoria ·
Restaurants in Italy are also trimming cats from the payroll, but six-year-old Marcello—laid off after his boss decided the restaurant didn't have a rodent problem after all—has adapted to his new situation with typical Continental flair. "It's okay. I peed on the fruit before I left," he says cheerfully.

Locked out · When Claire arrived for work at her usual time, she found that her boss had decamped without notice. "My last paycheck's in there! Does he think I'm supposed to get in through the mail slot, or what?" she asked with tears in her eyes.

·2·
No Cats Need Apply

Cats in the job jungle

◄◄ I thought you knew how it worked ·

"But how did the manual *get* stuck under the Enter key?"

◄ Buddy Juggles Jobs ·
"Maybe next time I should look for the incomplete job search handbook. That way I wouldn't have to hold up a big, huge book with both paws while I turn the pages with my tongue."

► Please mreow your mreow when you hear the mreeeeeow) ·
Delicat finally prevailed on her owner to let her record her own greeting on the household answering machine. "If someone really wants to hire me, they'll understand what I'm saying," she announced. "If they don't understand me, then the job wouldn't have been right for me anyway."

◄ Buddy makes a few job inquiries ·
Like so many other unemployed felines, Buddy now finds himself struggling to decipher job handbooks and want ads. "Why does a clinical psychologist get paid more than a laundromat attendant?" he frets here. "They're both advertised on the same page!"

◄ Counting the hours · "The head of Personnel was supposed to be back from lunch at two o'clock! I bet he's avoiding me. That bastard. There's no job for me there, and he knows it . . ."

▲ Phone stress · "I can't make this call. I just can't do it. I *know* they're not going to give me the job. Harry, can't you please call for me just this once?" "Okay, but this is *absolutely* the last time. Think about it—what kind of receptionist are you going to be if you can't even use the phone in your *own house?*"

◄ Typing the resume—first try · "It's lucky someone left a piece of paper in this, or I'd never be able to get started. Let's see. Do I say I'm married or single? Uh-oh, I pressed the equals sign. I'll have to start again."

▲ The thrill of the desktop resume · In mere moments, a middle-aged cat became a blur of activity when introduced to his owner's computer. "Look, I can even justify my columns!" he marveled. His finished resume contained thirteen different typefaces.

▲ Please, Mr. Postman, look and see if there's a letter, a letter for me · "It's *so* mortifying sitting out here where everyone can see me, but I just can't help myself. I only wish the mailman wouldn't chuck me under the goddam chin when he doesn't have a letter for me. What does he think—it cheers me up?"

► Please, Mr. Postman, make me feel better by leaving me a card or a letter · "Okay, Okay. I think the mailman is walking toward this house—oh, *no*, he's stopping at the Craigs' first. Okay, *now* he's coming toward us for sure. And his bag looks pretty heavy. I just know they wrote me about the job. I bet they want me to start on—Oh, God, oh God, he's just taking out *bills!* That's the *last* thing I need!"

Should I tweeze or not? · What to wear to the job interview is always a pressing problem. This Manhattan mother of ten finally decided that a simple white outfit with black and orange accents would work best. Unfortunately, she spent so much time worrying about her makeup that she missed the interview entirely. A shoddily groomed Himalayan got the job instead.

▲ Waiting in the Personnel Department ·

"I wish this guy next to me would stop clearing
his throat so much. He's trying to get the
receptionist's attention, I bet—he thinks she'll let
him go in first. Well, two can play at that game. I
bet he doesn't know how to whistle. I wonder
how fast he types. . . ."

▶ Stress interview · "I see your resume doesn't
list any activities for the first six months of last
year. Can you fill me in on that?"

·3·
Cat Counseling

God grant me the
courage to change
the things I can. . . .

◄◄ Hanging out with the gang · "It's kind of a—okay, I know it's a cliché—kind of a support group. Like we pass along job tips and help update each others' resumes and do practice interviews. Stuff like that. I always like to open the meeting with a little prayer—I guess that's what I was doing here."

▲ Private counseling · Creamsicle (left) parlayed a master's degree in social work into a lucrative career counseling unemployed cats. In the role-playing exercise shown here, Creamsicle impersonates a hostile boss trying to intimidate an employee. "The trouble is, I always start laughing. Which isn't great for the client, therapeutically speaking."

Go slow · Some cats find the counsel of other
species helpful. "You get what you pay for,"
comments an out-of-work cat actor whose
therapist is a box turtle. "I mean, the guy is, like,
fifty years old, so obviously he's had a lot of
experience. On the other hand, he's always late
to sessions—and half the time you can't even tell
whether he's in his office or not."

◄ Wisdom from a parrot · "Make sure to talk a lot," this career counselor advises a young ginger client. "That will make people think you're smart. Think you're smart! Think you're smart! Think you're smart! *Brawwwwk!*"

► Goat therapy · "I don't know why I keep coming to this guy. All he ever says is that butting people isn't the way to solve confrontations on the job—as though I had a *problem* with butting people in the first place!"

◄ Trading Places · *"I'm* the patient," snaps Minou (top) at a recent therapy session. "Why am *I* the one who has to sit up here in the basket? Let's trade places. I can't open up to you unless I'm lying on something upholstered."

◄ Your eyelids are getting heavy . . . · Ruddy took a friend's advice and went to a hypnotist to learn self-support techniques. "I guess his office is a little too comfortable. We *both* fell asleep. And then he had the gall to charge me for the session anyway!"

►I'm a client, not a salt lick · This cat was expecting resume-writing tips; he discovered to his horror that he had been mistakenly referred to a therapist whose specialty was "lingual massage." "I couldn't get out of there fast enough."

On the couch · "So I told that personnel director just what she could do with that catnip toy. And then *she* said, 'It sounds as though someone as hostile as you wouldn't work well in this company at all,' and I said . . . I said . . . You're not taking notes on this, are you? . . ."

The moment of truth · *"I knew* it! I knew you always fell asleep the minute I started talking!"

C'mon, feel the burn! · It's all too easy to let the pounds pile on when you're discouraged about your job prospects, so Molly (right) invested in a personal trainer. "You see all these unemployed cats whose stomachs start dragging on the ground. That's not going to happen to *me*."

· 4 ·
Home Chores and Other Horrors

The best thing about an office is that you don't have to change the storm windows

◄◄ Tax terror · "Don't you *dare* come near these receipts! I'll *faint* if you see what horrible records I kept. Oh, why didn't I hire an accountant while there was still time?"

◄ Catching up on chores at home · "There's this funny thing about bills that I never noticed while I was working—they just keep coming and coming. I mean, I pay them one month, and then the *next* month there's, like, this new huge stack of them all over again. What's the deal?"

◄ Keep the home fires burning · "They turned off the phone, but they can't turn off the heat, can they? That would be inhumane, wouldn't it? I mean, it's not my fault I can't pay the bills. They'll have to be patient, just the way *I* have to be patient."

April 15, Part 2 · "I'm not moving until you promise me that my trip to St. Kitts counts as a legitimate business expense."

▲ **April 15** · "If I just pretend I'm dead, someone else will *have* to finish my taxes for me."

QUICK QUESTIONS

▶ **Storming the IRS** · "I don't know if it's a quick question, really. It's just—what exactly *are* taxes?"

▶ Don't you need fingers to work one of these machines? · "Great. I wait and wait and wait in line to get the cash so I can pay my taxes, and of *course* the machine breaks when it's finally my turn."

▶ The check's in the mail · "You know, I've got things I need to *buy* with that refund. I bet that right this second someone else is getting that flea collar I saw at Saks."

▼ Down in the dregs · *"I* don't have a problem. It's not a problem when you have a couple of glasses of wine to help you relax in the afternoons. *You're* the one with the problem. You're always nagging me to go out and look for a job. Can't you see that kind of thing would make *any* cat drink?"

◄ Raiding the fridge · "Do you have to follow me around everywhere I *go?* I have a right to *eat* just like everyone *else* in this house! I suppose you're going to say that just because I'm not *contributing* to the family *finances* anymore, I should just go ahead and *starve* to death! For God's sake, get off my *back!"*

But what is there to wake up *for?* ·

Depression is common among jobless cats, many
of whom find themselves with no real reason to
get out of bed. "It's pathetic. I've gotten to the
point where I'm taking naps after *breakfast* now,"
reports Zara. "If anyone comes in, I sit up really
fast and pretend I'm thinking about something."

Crossing guard · To make ends meet,
Grover took a part-time job as a crossing guard.
"I nap a lot—it gives the kids more independence,
I think. Except the other day, this first-grader
walked into the street in front of a car, and boy!
I almost broke my back getting her onto the
sidewalk. Have *you* ever carried a fifty-pound
child by the scruff of the neck?"

Rabbit-sitting · "Oh, God. Their mother
didn't say anything about what to do if they
started playing doctor. Kids! Kids! Let's go inside
and make something with Legos, okay?"

▲ The joy of gardening · With extra time on their hands, some unemployed cats find themselves enjoying the simple pleasures of home more than ever before. "I can't believe I grew this myself," marvels Bette, a tiger cat from Nice. "And they taste so much better than houseplants!"

▶ Watering the vegetables · "I can't figure out how this thing works. You pick it up *here,* and the water comes out *here*—whoa! Yikes! Wait a minute! Damn, now I'll have to refill it."

▼ Let's see, what's this pound-y thing for? · The challenges of home carpentry fill the empty hours of many out-of-work cats. Dell, an ambitious amateur, decided to remodel his owners' entire house while they were on vacation. Unfortunately, they came home before he had quite figured out how to reassemble it. Here he listens anxiously as their car pulls into the driveway.

► Plastered · Asia, a tortoiseshell Persian, has become adept at plastering. "Don't tell anyone, but I walled my wire brush and my bladder medication up in there," she confides.

Painted into a corner · "Oh—uh—hi! We were—we were just—uh—cleaning up. I guess we spilled a little, huh? No problem, no problem. We'll have it out of your way in a jiffy. And—uh —by the way, you might not want to go into the living room for a couple of days. . . ."

Hey, Who Needs a Job?

Turns out there
are some advantages to
not working . . .

◄◄ *Qu'ils mangeant de la brioche* · "Let me tell you something," confides a cherished Manx. "I live pretty well. I never needed a job in the first place. I just did it because I thought females were supposed to. Now I can forget all that stupid 'work' stuff and go back to real life, thank God!"

▼ *Chic alors* · "One great thing is, since the buyout I've had way more time to work on my French. I think I'm starting to look more French, too. More *soignée*—that means well-groomed, you know. How's my accent?"

▲ Tickling the ivories · "Oh, I love to play the piano with my FEET *(pling! plang!)* Who cares if I have enough to EAT *(plonk! plonk!)* I just sing and dance all DAY *(bonk! bronk!)* Even though my money's gone AWAY *(prang! blonk!)*"

► Caught in the act · "Oh, don't be mad at us," beg the two youngest children of an out-of-work seamstress. "This is so much more fun than reading the want ads. And hey, maybe we'll work up some kind of twin-musician act and make it big!"

◄ Go for it! · The same drive that once made Zach the top salesman in his division is now channeled into sports at home. "That leaf is *mine*," he growls between clenched teeth. "I'm not gonna let some moron *tree* beat me!"

► Please pass the steroids · "You're supposed to roll this thing back and forth, right? . . . *Lift* it? No way. No one can do *that*. Anyway, I think I've done enough for today. It's best not to overdo at the beginning—you could get a rupture or something."

◄ Cattage industry · "I've come up with the most fabulous idea. Whisker-warmers! Can't you see it—each whisker wearing its own pretty little coat? I think it's a really hot concept. I bet I'll make way more than I ever did when I was a vice-principal."

► Artsy-catsy · Moonbeam relishes the chance to grow her own food ("Catch it, actually," she corrects a visitor) and revive forgotten crafts like spinning on her grandmother's old loom. What kind of yarn does she use? She blushes a bit at the question. "Uh—well, uh, actually—hairballs."

◄ Puzzled · "Jus' gimme one more second," mumbles Magpie at a recent puzzle tournament for cats. "I know I can . . . do it . . . the corner piece goes . . . uh . . . here . . . almos' done . . ."

▼ No contest · One of Magpie's competitors, a large male named Joshua, scoffs, " 'World's most difficult puzzle'—hah! I do *my* puzzles *upside-down!* Anyone who doesn't is a dog."

Couch counting · "When I get really desperate," Beau complains, "I count the dots on the slipcover. There are 14,753 in all, I think. I'll probably do a recount to make sure."

Gracious living · To boost her spirits, Demi
makes time for self-pampering rituals every day.
Afternoon tea in the dollhouse was her own idea.
"You can't love others until you begin to love the
child in yourself," she observes.

Vroom, vroom · "Don't tell Billy, but I set up his racecourse the minute he leaves for school," admits Shane, a seven-month-old shorthair. "The only trick is getting it all back in the box before he comes home."

▲**First choice of seats** · "Frankly, I don't understand why everyone doesn't decide to get fired. I'm always first in line now. Front-row seats for Harry Connick! Can you beat it?" Unfortunately, Willow was asked to leave shortly after this photo was taken; Connick is allergic to cats.

▶**Trouble in River City** · "What can you do? We've already seen every 'Love Boat' rerun three times. Plus the policeman who stops in here every day gives us pieces of his doughnut."

▶▶**Fry time** · "To hell with job hunting. I'm going to get a really great tan for once, and no one's going to stop me." I've always wanted to look like a ginger cat.

· 6 ·
Why Go Back to Work?

The lure of the open road,
where you never need
a litterbox

◄ ◄ Kitty biker · "This is definitely a fantastic way to see the world. I only wish it were a little easier to reach the handlebars."

◄ Cat rack · "I do think they might give me something a *little* more comfortable to ride in," frets a European bicolor on a French back road. "This is like sleeping on a subway grate."

◄ Vacances en voiture · "Okay, I admit it was nice of them to bring us along to Europe with them. But I don't see why we can't go into the museums along with them! It's not exactly stimulating sitting out here in the car—even if we *are* in a French parking lot."

► Roamin' Rome · "The view's best from the roof, and you don't get so many tourists up here, except for the rock-climbing types. Once I even foiled a burglary. This guy was stealing a woman's purse, and I jumped right down onto his head."

▲ Outward Bound · Pearl has come to view her enforced joblessness as a blessing in disguise. "I'm so much more self-reliant now. My survival skills are honed to the max. I could live in the wilderness for as long as I had to, except I don't really like the taste of squirrel."

▶ Waiting for the cowbirds to come home ·
"I'm working on making friends in the neighborhood," announces Fran from one of her favorite perches, "but sometimes it's tough. This bird family, for instance—they've never invited me in. They say it would be too expensive to have the door enlarged, but it sort of hurts my feelings."

◄ Goldfish for dinner · This Abbyssinian became an avid fisherman after taking early retirement. "The way you do it is, you get them to trust you," he explains, "talk about friends you have in common or something—and then move in for the kill. Not that different from business, come to think of it."

► Momming it up · Once a high-powered executive, Lilac now relishes the time she spends with her kittens. "I never realized you could tell them apart before," she says in wonder. "But they each have their own name and personality and everything! It's such an inspiration to me, the things you learn as a parent."

►► Fording the stream · "They let cats into the Olympics now, don't they?"

Docked · *"Don't tell anyone, but it doesn't actually bother me when it's too foggy to sail. I've never seen the point of staring at a bunch of water."*

Off to Edgartown · For a cat, there's
something very special about a seaside vacation.
Here, two friends wait eagerly for the Woods
Hole ferry that will bring them to the summer
house they share on Martha's Vineyard.
"I can't wait to taste fresh seagull again,"
exults Newton (left).

◄ Choosing the perfect shades · Many felines flee to warmer climes in winter. Here, Pumpkin agonizes over the choice of sunglasses offered at a shop in Vero Beach. "I don't care that much about UV protection or anything. What I'd really like is something that goes with my bracelets."

Toiletry · "Do you *mind?* I just happen to
like sand better than kitty litter—is that a problem
for you?"

◄ Camouflage · This Silver-Shaded Persian used to be a Chocolate Persian until she toured Alaska. "I like to make that little extra effort to match my surroundings. There's no point in letting your standards down just because you're free-lancing. Besides"—she giggles—"there's an Arctic fox I'm kind of interested in. . . ."

▲ Winter fashions · "Tweeds has fantastic stuff for cats. Well, it's for people really, but you can have it altered. I had my dressmaker fix up one of their leg warmers to make this sweater here."

►► Life on the Soft Track · "You know, maybe it's time for me to face the fact that life off the fast track just isn't that bad."